# DARE
## TO BE
# BOLD!

### A 31 Day Devotional

# DARE
## TO BE
# BOLD!
### A 31 DAY DEVOTIONAL

## NERY STONE

PAGE
TURNER
BOOKS INC.

Henderson, NV, USA

Dare to Be Bold!, 1st Edition.
Story concept © 2024 by Nery Stone.
Original editing and print preparation © 2024 Staback Author Services
Cover art and back cover summary by Leanne E. Staback, Ph.D.
(See Bibliography for downloaded artwork used on cover and interior).

Books may be ordered through popular, online retailers, Page Turner Books, Inc.'s online store, or by contacting the publisher at:

PAGE TURNER BOOKS, INC.
170 S. GREEN VALLEY PKWY., STE. 300
HENDERSON, NV 89012-3145

Visit our website at www.ptbooksinc.com or
contact us via email at contact@ptbooksinc.com (Secondary email:
ptbooksinc@outlook.com – please email to both addresses)

Page Turner Books, Inc.'s name and logo are copyright of Page Turner Books, Inc.
ISBN: 978-1-958487-13-6 (Paperback Edition)
Printed in the United States of America.
First Hardcover Printing: July 2024
Library of Congress Control Number: 2024936510

---

**ATTENTION CORPORATIONS AND ORGANIZATIONS:**
Most Page Turner Books, Inc. books are available at quantity discounts with bulk purchase for educational, business, or sales promotional use. For information, please call or write:

**Special Markets Department, Page Turner Books, Inc.**
**170 S. Green Valley Pkwy., Ste. 300, Henderson, NV 89012**
**Telephone: (702) 606-1775**

# Dedication

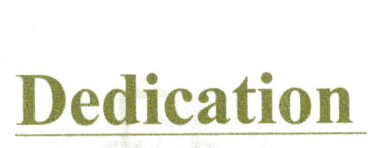

God has allowed me the opportunity to serve, and I cannot be more grateful. I've been blessed beyond measure. I am dedicating this book to my three children: Antonio, Ruth and Angel, who were dragged from church to church and never complained. I thank them for their patience and love. Remember, "the seed that was planted in you and that without God, we can do nothing."

Dear Reader:

This collection of daily messages was written to encourage you to live life to the fullest in spite of the many bumps in the road we encounter every day. If you are fainthearted, these words come filled with strength, hope, peace, joy, and love. They are intended to make you smile and laugh more often, to build you up and take you to your utmost potential, and to inspire you to walk with your head held high - not in arrogance, but humbly knowing who you are in Christ.

We only have ONE LIFE—let's live it!

In John 10:10, Jesus said, *"The thief comes only to steal and kill and destroy; I have come that they may have life and have it to the full."*

Enjoy each thought for every day of the month, walking the talk and bringing others along as you shine in this world of darkness.

~Nery Stone

# Day 1

And The Clock Goes…
"Tick, Tock, Tick,
Tock!"

Our day could be described in so many ways:

- ✠ A new beginning
- ✠ The day the Lord has made
- ✠ The first day of a new month
- ✠ A day we've never lived before

Whatever the description looks like, we are encouraged to value the time we've been given.

- ✠ Use it wisely
- ✠ Use it to be a blessing to someone
- ✠ Live as though the day was our last
- ✠ Love like we've never loved before

*Psalm 139:14 says that you've been "fearfully and wonderfully made."*

Let's forgive freely, quickly, and eagerly because each of us is in need of that same forgiveness every single day.

## <u>Prayer for Day 1</u>

*God,*

*Help me to trust you and to give others the same grace you have granted me so that at the end of the day, I will have enjoyed today's "tick, tock!"*

*In Jesus' name I pray,*

*Amen.*

# How have I embraced Today's "Tick-Tock"?

_____

_____

_____

_____

_____

_____

_____

_____

_____

_____

# Day 2

Feeling Stuck…?

Life can sometimes feel like the childhood song by James Orchard Halliwell "Here We Go Round the Mulberry Bush". Around and around and around in the same circle, same place, same everything, day after day, week after week. Soon enough those weeks turn into months, which turn into years...

Wait a minute! Shake yourself! Listen!

Today is a new opportunity to venture outside of your "mulberry bush" and actually take a step forward. Let's do something we've never done before. Let's challenge ourselves!

Let's look in the mirror and see the jewels we are. Let's shine in the corner of the world where God has placed us. Let's be confident, and at the end of the day, tell our mulberry bush, "See you later, alligator!"

## <u>Prayer for Day 2</u>

*God,*

*I feel stuck in every possible way. It feels like I am no longer making progress, and just spinning around in circles. I know that life doesn't always make sense, and that I need to turn to You for help. Please guide me.*

*In Jesus' name I pray,*

*Amen.*

# How do I feel stuck today?

_____

_____

_____

_____

_____

_____

_____

_____

_____

_____

# Day 3

A Reminder…
We are Loved!

We all pursue love and happiness. We want to be acknowledged, recognized, and appreciated. Our search takes us down many paths and avenues, some of which lead us to make wrong choices and decisions based on emotional impulse. This can leave us with broken hearts, heaps of frustration, and feelings of despair.

However, our Father looks down from His throne at our human attempts that result in failure upon failure and tries to tell us, "I'm here; I've proven my love for you by sending My very best Gift, my Son."

He paid for our redemption with His life, and every day the Holy Spirit reminds us of that ONE constant:

His love that transcends all barriers, not only for this season of our lives, but now and throughout eternity — time without end.

Let's walk in that love today.

It's with us on the mountain tops, and even more so, in the valleys—a constant reminder: "I love you!"

# <u>Prayer for Day 3</u>

*Dear Lord,*

*There may come a time when the world ceases to exist, Lord; but I know that your love for me will never end. Your love is unconditional, your mercies never end, and your faith in me is great! For this, I am thankful.*

*In Jesus' name I pray,*

*Amen.*

# How did I feel God's love today?

_____

_____

_____

_____

_____

_____

_____

_____

_____

_____

# Day 4

## Chains of Unforgiveness – Break Them Today!

No one enjoys getting hurt, but because we are still on this broken planet we must understand that getting hurt is unavoidable.

However, it's how we react to it—how we handle it—that makes all the difference in the world.

We can either choose to live the rest of our days feeding the pain with negativity, resentment, grudges, and bitterness, continuing to bring the past into every conversation; *or* we can decide to get up, wipe the tears, take a hot shower, and understand that life is too short, and those things only make it even shorter.

Let's move forward with a smile on our face and peace in our hearts. The Scriptures tell us:

*"And forgive us our sins, for we also forgive everyone who is indebted to us."*
(Luke 11:4)

Again, because this issue is so important, we can either bury the past, enjoy a good night's rest, and live in the fullness of joy; *or* we can remain with hands and feet tied to the hurts of the past.

For mental and emotional sanity, today is a good day for us to walk in love and forgiveness.

# Prayer for Day 4

*Dear Heavenly Father,*

*Help me learn to forgive others and let go of the past, so I can move forward to the future. Please forgive me for not being forgiving, for holding grudges, wishing evil upon others, and hoping for revenge.*

*Amen.*

# Whom have I *not* forgiven; and how is it affecting me?

_____

_____

_____

_____

_____

_____

_____

_____

_____

_____

# Day 5

## When Grandma is in the House

Do we realize how blessed we are if we are a grandma?

*"May you live to see your children's children…"*
(Psalm 128:6)

How awesome that is!

As we look into the eyes of our descendants, what a miracle it is to see a part of ourselves in them to carry out our legacy! Let's enjoy them and make precious memories. Let's do for them what we were unable to do for our sons and daughters.

Show affection; they love and yearn for our hugs and kisses. Bake their favorite pies, cakes, and cookies. Let's be their greatest fans and the loudest voice at their performances. When grandma is around, tears turn into laughter; the pain from falls and bruises easily and swiftly disappear.

"I cannot" turns into "I can."

All this (and much more) happens when Grandma is in the house.

# <u>Prayer for Day 5</u>

*Lord God,*

*Bless our grandparents with long lives, happiness and good health. May they remain steadfast in your love and be earthly guides to their children and grandchildren, as signs of your presence.*

*In Jesus' name I pray,*

*Amen.*

# What do I love about being a grandparent; or what do I love about my grandparents?

_____

_____

_____

_____

_____

_____

_____

_____

_____

_____

# Day 6

# Have You Smelled the Roses Lately?

We would enjoy our lives much more if we only slowed down! Sometimes we have to say NO to all the hustle and bustle the road of life throws at us. Our to-do list may grow to be as long as Pinocchio's nose, creating unnecessary stress, and we can forget that we only have one life to live.

We need to set boundaries in place for ourselves with the people around us.

## SLOW DOWN!

## PRIORITIZE!

# GET ORGANIZED!

Whatever does not get done today will be waiting for us tomorrow morning.

When was the last time we told a family member or friend how much we love them, that we're thinking of them or praying for them?

These are the little things that allow us to stop and smell the roses with those who are dear to us.

## <u>Prayer for Day 6</u>

*Dear Lord,*

*Please help me get out of this cycle of stress. Give me the strength needed to say "no" to the temptation of trying to do it all. Guide me in your wisdom in every decision, letting you take the reins, instead of me trying to do it all myself. Help me remember that all things are possible with you, if only I would allow my faith in you to flow freely. Thank you for being powerful in my weakness, and faithful through my struggles. I love you and ask for you to provide me with peace and less stress.*

*In Jesus' name I pray,*

*Amen.*

# What are my priorities (and what can wait until tomorrow)?

_____

_____

_____

_____

_____

_____

_____

_____

_____

_____

# Day 7

## Our Journey, What Does It Look Like?

God's Word says,

*"By faith Abraham obeyed when he was called to go out to the place which he would receive as an inheritance.*
*And he went out, not knowing where he was going."*

(Hebrews 11:8)

Can we relate? We don't always understand what's going on around us. Surrounded by chaos and unanswered questions, we are often left with no other option but to trust that God is in control.

In our day-to-day adventure, we have no time to entertain defeat, failure, or self-pity. We know that our identity is hidden in Christ and...

*"...all things work together for good."*
(Romans 8:28)

Let's continue to look up and strive to please God by living by faith and expecting

Him to come through on every promise. At the end, we'll be able to say:

> *"I have fought the good fight,*
> *I have finished the race,*
> *I have kept the faith.*
> *Finally, there is laid up for me*
> *the crown of righteousness,*
> *which the Lord,*
> *the righteous Judge,*
> *will give to me on that Day..."*
> (2 Timothy 4:7-8)

# <u>Prayer for Day 7</u>

*Dear Lord,*

*Help me each day to find faith in the midst of chaos. Give me the desire to seek you when times are tough; and the ability to see you, hear you, talk to you, and give thanks to you in times of trouble or stress.*

*Amen.*

# What do I do to please God?

_____

_____

_____

_____

_____

_____

_____

_____

_____

_____

# Day 8

## He's Got You!

Remember this childhood poem by Lewis Carroll?

"Humpty Dumpty, sat on a wall.
Humpty Dumpty had a great fall.
All the King's horses,
And all the King's men,
Couldn't put Humpty together again."

That is definitely NOT our story!

*"Though the righteous fall seven times,
they rise again..."*
(Proverbs 24:16)

*"The Lord upholds all who fall and lifts up
all who are bowed down."*
(Psalms 145:14)

What a comfort! What a blessed assurance that we are in the palm of His hand! He promises to be with us always, in every circumstance. No matter what comes our way, He remains the infallible God, the beginning and the end, the one who changes not, the one who holds our future.

Do not fear what may come your way—

He's got you!

# Prayer for Day 8

*Dear Lord,*

*Compared to your sacrifice, my brokenness seems small; but the emotional pain feels overwhelming. I come to you, seeking solace and healing. I give myself over to your gentle embrace, and trust that you will restore my soul.*

*In Jesus' name,*

*Amen.*

# What fears have I turned over to God?

_____

_____

_____

_____

_____

_____

_____

_____

_____

_____

_____

# Day 9

# Birds of a Feather…

What voices are we listening to?

Who do we spend time with on a frequent basis?

Are they bringing the best out of us, or are they sinking us deeper into the pit of despair?

We are the apple of God's eye. We are loved, gifted, and highly favored, more than conquerors. We are blessed more than we can imagine; but to remain blessed, we must be very selective of whom we allow to enter our circle of influence. Wrong choices will reap dreadful consequences, for everything we sow has a harvest.

We are deceived if we think that we can hang out with the wrong crowd without being influenced by what they do and say. That is simply not true. They will change the way we think, speak, and act.

Misery loves company, birds of a feather *do* flock together!

Choose wisely to be happy.

# Prayer for Day 9

*Dear Lord,*

*Please help me to surround myself with good people, relationships ordained by you. Thank you for the courage and grace to let go of detrimental friendships and seek healthy ones.*

*Amen.*

# What relationships are harming my relationship with God?

_____

_____

_____

_____

_____

_____

_____

_____

_____

_____

# Day 10

## Battling with Rejection

We fight an unseen enemy and face battles every day.

Our rest at night may even be disturbed by nightmares or depression stemming from rejection.

Have you been there?

Have you been bombarded by thoughts such as:
- ✤ "I don't fit in."
- ✤ "I don't like how I look."
- ✤ "I don't live in the nice neighborhood."
- ✤ "I still drive the same old broken-down car that's always in the mechanic's shop."
- ✤ "I have no diplomas hanging on the walls."
- ✤ "No one wants to hear what I have to say."

✝ "Nobody loves me…"

Please believe that there is GOOD NEWS today!

Let's lift our heads, check our posture, and put a smile on our faces. And guess what? We are not alone.

*"He came to His own, and His own did not receive Him."*
(John 1:11 says concerning Jesus)

Rejection did not stop Him from fulfilling His mission, and the same applies to us. Don't stop, don't quit, don't give up. Let's go, moving forward, never looking back. Friends will leave, sometimes even family members will walk away, but HIS love for you is unconditional…never failing, constant, and consistent.

In good times and bad times, He never stops loving us.

*"…there is a friend who sticks closer than a brother."*

(Proverbs 18:24)

# <u>Prayer for Day 10</u>

*Thank you, Lord, for never casting me aside. You accept me just the way I am. Renew my mind so the root of rejection will no longer manifest itself in my life in the form of anger, bitterness, perfectionism, or despair. It is broken through your blood.*

*Amen.*

# Ways I have felt God's love:

_____

_____

_____

_____

_____

_____

_____

_____

_____

_____

# Day 11

## The Unknown Future

We most likely began the day with a calendar that is overflowing with many appointments and a long list of things to do; however, yesterday there was no guarantee we were going to wake up this morning.

So how do we deal with the uncertainty each day brings?

*First*, we must understand that we are frail and flawed creatures, deeply loved by the heavenly Father. He demonstrated this on the cross through His Son Jesus when He said, *"It is finished."*

We are maintained and sustained by the Holy Spirit who lives within us.

*Second*, we owe our existence to a Higher Power and a relationship with God. He guarantees a peace that surpasses all human logic, especially if we've surrendered our lives to Him.

He is the "glue" that keeps it all together.

Tomorrow is no longer a worry or a concern because the unknown future is in the hands of a known God. He's got our backs!

## <u>Prayer for Day 11</u>

*Dear Lord,*

*I am worried about my future. I am often unsatisfied with how my life has gone. I know this is not good for my relationship with you. I have failed to praise you for the many blessings I have received from you. I forget to look at all the good I have in life, even though I know it can disappear in the blink of an eye. I don't want to live the rest of my life living in the past...but in the present, since each new day is a gift. I pray that I remember to follow you into the future, and that your will and glory be done in my life. I love and trust you with all my heart.*

*In Jesus' name,*

*Amen.*

# Worries I have about tomorrow:

_____

_____

_____

_____

_____

_____

_____

_____

_____

_____

# Day 12

The Gift of Life

Take a quiet moment for inner reflection and look to the sky. No matter what the weather is, recognize that it's a beautiful day because we are alive!

I was in a restaurant having breakfast, and someone looked around and said, "Let's celebrate the people who survived COVID-19!" We lifted our glasses, made a toast in honor of our fellow citizens, and expressed sincere gratitude for still being counted among the living.

We are the recipients of so many blessings every day—some we are not even aware of. We should take nothing for granted and lift our thoughts to Him constantly throughout the day, acknowledging His goodness, mercy, and grace.

Place your hand over the upper left-hand side of your chest and feel your heartbeat.

We are alive—alive to serve Him, alive to love Him, and alive to thank Him for His faithfulness!

## Prayer for Day 12

*Dear Lord,*

*Today I have received your blessing of the gift of life, good health, food and shelter. I have been blessed with warmth from the sun, peace, and a thankful heart. Even though many may not see it as a special day, I have enjoyed it as another day full of blessings. Let me not forget the beauty of the gift of life.*

*In Jesus' name,*

*Amen.*

# Blessings I have received:

_____

_____

_____

_____

_____

_____

_____

_____

_____

_____

# Day 13

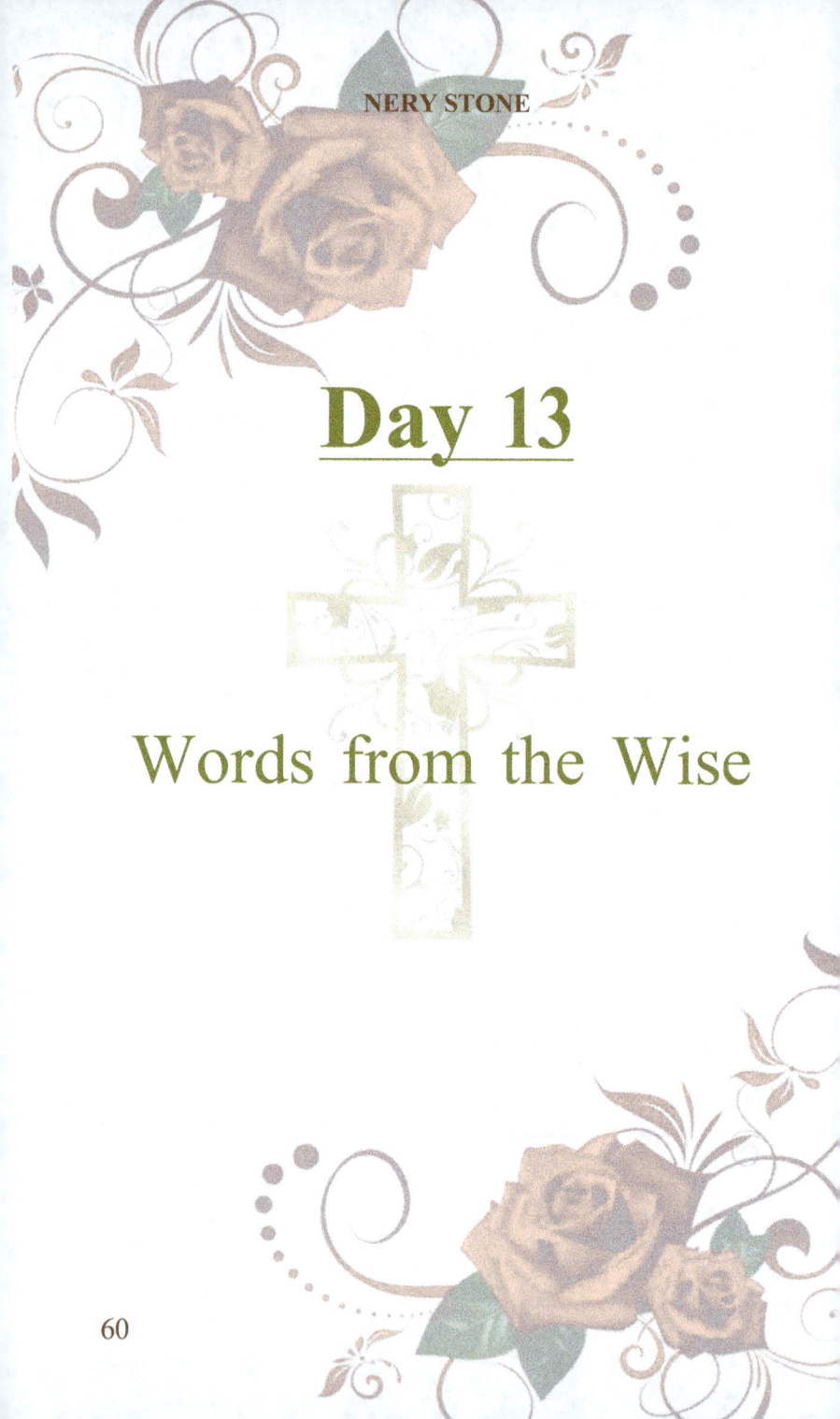

# Words from the Wise

Some folks have been on the planet longer than us, so their counsel and experience are worth their weight in gold.

Parents and grandparents would love for their children to avoid falling into the pitfalls of life or shedding tears of pain and disappointment; but that is not realistic.

Everyone has their own story to write and to live; however, the hope is that they will heed the advice wrapped in love and genuine care by their elders.

As I was growing up, my mother would share how she always pursued friendships and relationships with older women who taught her how to be a good wife and prepare meals for the family. She learned how to clean the fish that she bought directly from the fishermen who caught it at sea and how to properly clean chicken at the central market.

Let's treasure these golden nuggets that come from the mouths of the wise; they are jewels and truths no longer welcome; but oh, how much the world needs them!

# Prayer for Day 13

*Dear Lord,*

*I ask that you bless my elders with wisdom, patience and grace. Let them be encouraging and an inspiration to all who seek their knowledge. May they continue to share their wisdom and knowledge with others for many years to come, leaving a positive legacy for younger generations.*

*In Jesus' name,*

*Amen.*

# What advice have I received from my elders?

_____

_____

_____

_____

_____

_____

_____

_____

_____

_____

# Day 14

It Took a Miracle

John W. Peterson wrote:

> "It took a miracle
> to put the stars in place.
> It took a miracle
> to hang the world in space.
> But when He saved my soul,
> Cleansed and made me whole,
> It took a miracle of love and grace."

Let our choice today be to maintain a positive perspective about life, in spite of whatever trial we go through, and whatever challenge we face.

We are not victims. Rather, we are victors without time for pity parties or feeling sorry for ourselves. We walk in the victory and freedom Christ paid for on the cross.

Let's wake up every morning with gratitude because many will never wake from their sleep.

With that mindset, we'll be totally surprised by what the Lord has done. There will be no other choice but to turn our frowns into smiles! Our creation and everything about it is nothing short of a miracle.

# Prayer for Day 14

*Dear Lord,*

*As I awake on this new day, I come before you filled with gratitude. Thank you for today and the opportunities it brings. Please guide me in all I do today.*

*In Jesus' name,*

*Amen.*

# What negative things have occurred in my life, and what positives came out of it?

_____

_____

_____

_____

_____

_____

_____

_____

_____

# Day 15

# What Do You See?

It's been said that beauty is in the eye of the beholder. What a blessing it is to have the gift of sight!

It is, however, very easy to point out the flaws and mistakes of others because that is what we choose to see.

Why not do the opposite? Let's choose to see the good, the kindness, and the love in others.

*"...whatever things are true,*
*whatever things are noble,*
*whatever things are just,*
*whatever things are pure,*
*whatever things are lovely,*
*whatever things are of good report,*
*if there is any virtue and if there is*
*anything praiseworthy –*
*meditate on these things."*
(Philippians 4:8)

If we change our mindset, we'll realize that we can achieve longer and more restful sleep, and our lives will be much more relaxing and fulfilling.

Remember that we are on this planet to be difference makers and world changers, but that difference and that change starts with us.

# Focus on one person you find flawed and write about the *good* things that person offers.

_____

_____

_____

_____

_____

_____

_____

_____

_____

## <u>Prayer for Day 15</u>

*Dear Lord,*

*Help me to see the beauty, dignity, and your image in others, way more clearly, than I see their faults and brokenness. When I see weakness in others, I pray that you help me to view them with compassion and understanding – not with frustration and irritation. Help me to see what you see in my family members, friends, coworkers, and even strangers.*

*In Jesus' name,*

*Amen.*

# Day 16

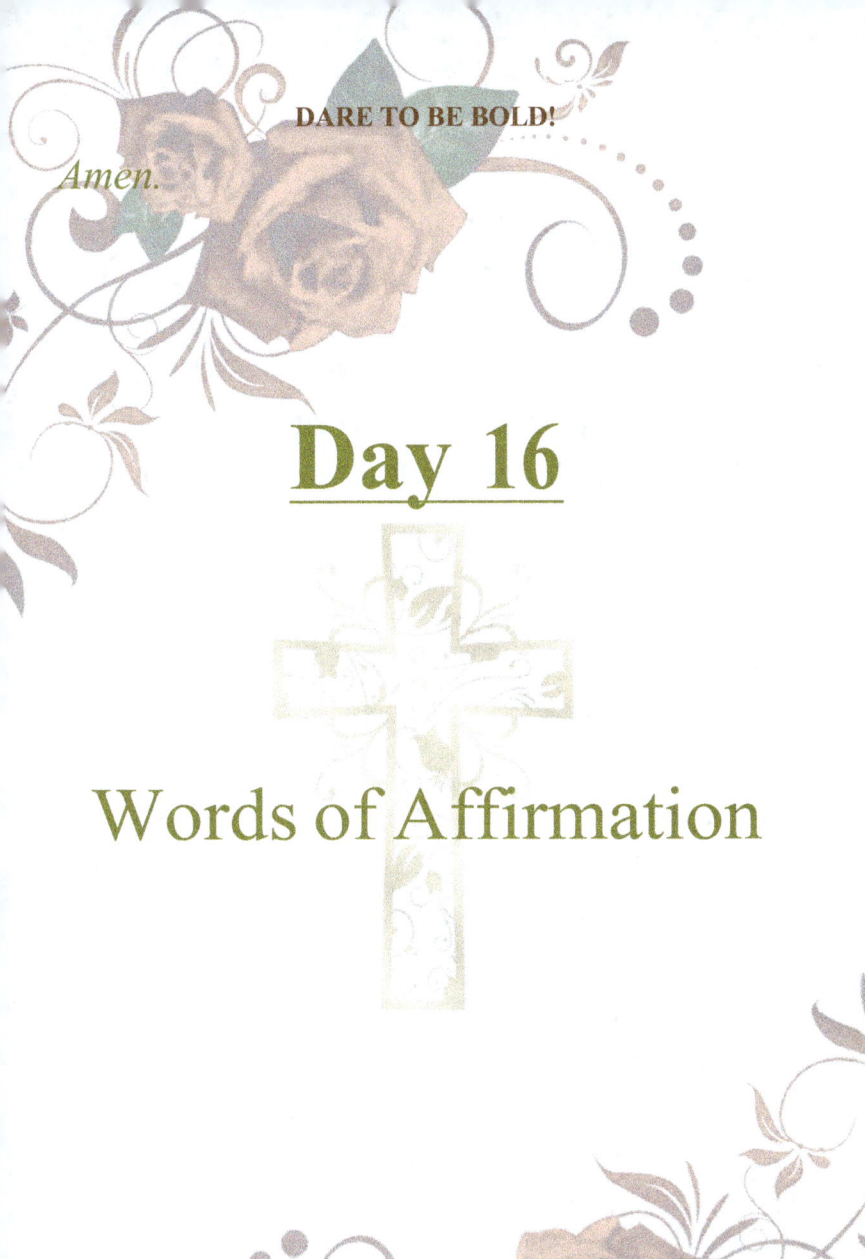

# Words of Affirmation

Words of affirmation are not spoken enough, and we desperately need the encouragement they bring. In our respective circle of influence, we should not end a day without having told someone how nice they look, that we're praying for them, or reminding them that the best is yet to come.

We should strive to be a motivation to those around us, focusing on each other's talents rather than our shortcomings. What we think is what we will speak, so it's important to carefully consider the thoughts that enter our mind.

We should be sure to immediately discard all negative and destructive thoughts, casting them out of our minds. If we don't do this and allow them to grow in our heart, declaration and execution will follow.

Make a list of words of affirmation that you can speak to yourself daily then to others.

Let it be a habit that you cultivate. Let's ask the Holy Spirit to give us the mind of Christ so that what flows from our lips will not only be pleasing to Him but a blessing to others.

# <u>Prayer for Day 16</u>

*Dear Lord,*

*Please provide your love, grace and guidance in the words I speak to those I should meet today. I pray for your strength and wisdom.*

*In Jesus' name I pray,*

*Amen.*

# Daily words of affirmation for me and others:

_____

_____

_____

_____

_____

_____

_____

_____

_____

_____

# Day 17

## 65 Plus…

It would appear that many who are approaching, or are in, retirement look at it as a bleak time to resist for as long as they can. This might be caused by the expectation of a declining quality of life with the use of a walker or wheelchair, a multiplicity of doctor appointments, and boxes full of pills which need to be color-coded lest we endanger ourselves.

However, retirement is *NOT* the expectation of being unable to think and act for yourself.

It's *NOT* the expectation to sleep the rest of your days away. To the contrary, it should *BE* the season of life when you regain control of the clock, the calendar, the schedule.

It's the time to enjoy people and things that being in the workforce did not allow.

It's the time to do crazy and unplanned

things that make us and others laugh, that inspire others many times on the spur of the moment.

A time to be *YOU*, for *YOU*, to breathe and have fun. What better time to live the abundant life that Christ has given us?

If retirement is something you've been dreading, change that mindset *NOW*!

## <u>Prayer for Day 17</u>

*Dear Lord,*

*I pray that retirement will be a new beginning for me. Help me not to view it as the end of the road, as many do when retirement age arrives. Please help me to be aware of new opportunities as they appear, and to use skills and gifts you have given me, so they may be used to glorify your name.*

*In Jesus' name,*

*Amen.*

# When I retire, I am looking forward to…

_____

_____

_____

_____

_____

_____

_____

_____

_____

_____

# Day 18

I Do…

These are two very important words spoken by the bride and groom, but how seriously are they taken?

Wedding vows need to be thought through with careful consideration. They are meant to be a commitment that should last until death.

This is because we:

*First*, have invited God to be the center (the "glue") of our relationship.

*Second*, because we have surrendered our selfishness to each other.

Marriage is beyond physical beauty because it is not eternal. It's defined by two people who have decided to share their journey on planet earth, navigating the school of life when there are rainbows in the sky, *AND* when they face valleys.

Many people spend thousands of dollars on an event that, unfortunately, ends in divorce court where children are forced to choose who they will spend Thanksgiving dinner with.

May this not be our lot in life because we've prayerfully sought God's will before we say the words "I do."

# Prayer for Day 18

*Father,*

*I ask that you give my spouse and I the ability to be a united front for you, letting nothing come between us. Help us to identify and work through those things that are not pleasing to you so we can reach solid unity in our marriage in all ways. I love you and thank you for all of these things.*

*In Jesus' name,*

*Amen.*

# How has your marital commitment to God changed over the years?

_____

_____

_____

_____

_____

_____

_____

_____

_____

# Day 19

## Life is
## Not a Dream…

In 1852, an author and teacher, Eliphalet Oram Lyte, wrote this familiar folk tune:

"Row, row, row your boat,
Gently down the stream.
Merrily, merrily, merrily, merrily,
Life is but a dream."

Do you have fond childhood memories of being rocked to sleep to this familiar tune? During our toddler years, it would appear that life is indeed a dream—all needs are met, and we live in a bubble of rainbows and Skittles™.

However, as the years go by and we grow up, we arrive at the rude awakening that life is no longer a dream. We have to get out of bed early to go to school then do homework; we realize that along with our needs, there are also wants that are no longer freely given by parents or guardians, so we find ourselves joining the working class to pay bills.

We must face challenges while understanding that we do not live in a fairytale castle where a genie grants our every wish.

Life takes us through many hills and valleys. While it's not always a dream, dreams can come true. It's our call, our choice, our decision if, when, and how soon they do.

# <u>Prayer for Day 19</u>

*Dear Lord,*

*I feel like I am growing up in an unsteady and confusing world. Please reveal your plans for my life so that I may follow the path you have created for me. Help me take failure as a chance for a new start. Give me strength to hold my faith in you and keep alive my joy in your creation.*

*In Jesus' name,*

*Amen.*

# What dreams of mine have come true?

_____

_____

_____

_____

_____

_____

_____

_____

_____

_____

# Day 20

## Do You Know Who You Are?

A farmer bought an eagle egg and put it in a chicken coop. As the baby eagle grew, it did everything the chickens did. They were very sociable; they liked to stay busy in groups as they roamed looking for bugs and grubs. They loved to search for worms!

The baby eagle made the same noises chickens do and flew only a certain distance like chickens do. In this story, the eagle did not know it was an eagle that could soar.

Do we know who *WE* are? What are our short and long-term goals? Where do we see ourselves in five years?

We do not have to remain a product of our environment.

## Let's be bold and courageous!

# Let's make things happen against all odds!

We need to be true to ourselves and be all that we can be for such a time as this.

It takes six to eight people to lift our casket when we die. Imagine the possibilities if those six to eight people were to lift us while we are alive.

*"They will soar high on wings like eagles. They will run and not grow weary. They will walk and not faint."*
*(Isaiah 40:31)*

## <u>Prayer for Day 20</u>

*Dear Lord,*

*Let me see that I am thriving. May I rejoice in you and your guidance. Show me that my successes are blessings from you, and answers to my prayers. Above all, I will put my trust in you and your unconditional love.*

*In Jesus' name,*

*Amen.*

# Jot down three of your short-term goals, and one long term goal:

_____

_____

_____

_____

_____

_____

_____

_____

_____

_____

# Day 21

# Do it Now!

Catch the moment and embrace it; it's fleeting.

Sometimes, we try to do a "repeat" of the times that follow; but there are some that are "once-in-a-lifetime" occurrences. If we miss them, there is no next time, and we are left with a multitude of regrets.

For example, someone is at the beach drowning, and the lifeguard shouts, "The wave is coming! Jump in it!" This is the kind of instruction that is given only once, so we must obey it immediately or end up six feet under.

The sayings that *"Procrastination is the thief of time"* and *"Don't leave for tomorrow what you can do today"* are so real because life is so short. Let's always be in the moment, showing appreciation, love, kindness, and encouragement.

# <u>Prayer for Day 21</u>

*Dear Lord,*

*I ask you to fill me with your Holy Spirit, so that whatever needs to be done in my life today, will be done by Your power    and strength working in and through me.*

*In Jesus Name I pray,*

*Amen!"*

# Moments I have been glad I didn't procrastinate:

_____

_____

_____

_____

_____

_____

_____

_____

_____

_____

# Day 22

# The Lighthouse

Most fishermen will tell you that they use the lighthouse as a backup for electronic equipment.

A lighthouse also serves to warn of dangerous shallows and rocky coasts.

A lighthouse defeats the darkness.

The Scriptures tell us that we are the light of the world, bringing the hope of salvation through Christ to a world desperately in need of a Savior.

How do we shine?

As the saying goes "actions speak louder than words", so we shine through our deeds, always showing grace, mercy, and love. Light cannot be hidden. We have to make the conscious decision to show the love of God and speak hope into the lives of others.

Be the difference the world so desperately needs.

## <u>Prayer for Day 22</u>

*Dear Lord,*

*I have learned your ways of light. Help me to be the light in this world which is so flawed. Let your light shine through my life; and show me how to live that my work may be your work, performed in your ways, so that others can see and feel your light through me.*

*In Jesus' name,*

*Amen.*

# How do my actions show grace, mercy and love?

_____

_____

_____

_____

_____

_____

_____

_____

_____

_____

# Day 23

## Make Some Noise

It's said that the squeaky wheel gets the attention; but due to a lack of self-confidence, we often allow depression, negativity, and our own insecurities to back us into a corner and keep our mouths shut.

Please know that your voice must be heard.

Everyone has a personal story that can certainly make an impact on someone else's life.

We must be diligent, direct, and determined to share our successes as well as our failures with others. This might encourage or comfort someone who is experiencing the same pain as us, motivating them to move forward while avoiding the mistakes we've already made.

**DARE TO BE BOLD!**

# Speak up!

# Get up!

# Look up!

# <u>Prayer for Day 23</u>

*Dear Lord,*

*Please guide me to share my stories so that you are present in each and every one of them. By sharing my faith, I want people to know that you are ever-present, ever faithful, and the ever-loving guide on this journey called life on earth. I want non-believers to hear my stories in such a way that they might turn to you. Show me those who need to connect with you and fill my mouth with the words THEY need to hear.*

*In Jesus' name,*

*Amen.*

# My successes and failures to share with others in need:

_____

_____

_____

_____

_____

_____

_____

_____

_____

_____

# Day 24

Ouch! It Hurts!

It has been said: "When your dog bites you, you are well bitten!"

We can only imagine the pain Jesus felt when he was betrayed by one of his closest disciples, Judas Iscariot—a betrayal sealed with a kiss! So if anyone understands that hurt, He does!

This thought takes us to a fact many don't want to accept *people change.*

Judas did not entertain deception when he was first called to follow Jesus and later assigned as treasurer of the group. It was over a time—taking a coin here and there for personal use, lying here and there—that took him deeper, which culminated in Jesus being arrested, whipped, crowned with thorns, and ultimately crucified on Mount Calvary.

Can we relate in any way to the hurt of loved ones keeping their distance, choosing to hang out with others, and leaving us behind?

Yes, it hurts, but love cannot be forced.

That's why John 3:16 is clear when it says,

"For God so loved the world that He gave His only begotten Son, *that whosoever believes in Him* should not perish but have everlasting life."

It's a choice!

## <u>Prayer for Day 24</u>

*Dear Lord,*

*Please give me the power to forgive by letting go of the offense and trusting that you will bring justice to those who have harmed me. Free me from the burden of holding a grudge so that I can move on with my life. I confess that this betrayal has damaged me to the core. I lay this situation in your hands, so that I may move on and continue to live my life according to your plan.*

*In Jesus' name,*

*Amen.*

# Grudges I am holding on to:

_____

_____

_____

_____

_____

_____

_____

_____

_____

# Day 25

## Give Someone a Chance

Unfortunately, we do not invest the time to really get to know who a person is from the inside out; but rather, we unjustly choose to build walls and distance ourselves as a result of unfair judgements of the outward appearance.

When people don't meet our expectations, we forbid them from making any efforts toward building a loving relationship. We deliberately refuse them the opportunity to display their talents and gifts. And most importantly, we refuse to find out why God has allowed them to enter into our lives.

Could it be that they were sent to bless us; but because they do not fit our ideals, we've let the blessing pass us by?

Let's take inventory; let's be honest with ourselves and answer the question: "Who are we pushing away?"

## <u>Prayer for Day 25</u>

*Dear Lord,*

*I find that I am turning potential friends away because I have been so guarded about people based on appearances. Please help me to look beyond a person's physical appearance, and into the heart and soul of a person so that I am not pushing away those whom I need in my life.*

*In Jesus' name I pray,*

*Amen.*

# People whom I have rejected because of their appearance:

_____

_____

_____

_____

_____

_____

_____

_____

_____

_____

# Day 26

Beauty for Ashes

Because Adam and Eve disobeyed God's command, sin and all its ugliness entered the world.

As a consequence of this, there are many sights that are unpleasant to behold:
- ✝ Human Deformities
- ✝ Sickness
- ✝ Murder
- ✝ War
- ✝ Kidnapping
- ✝ Imprisonment, and so much more.

However, in the midst of all of the above, there is beauty in creation. God has poured out beauty through His spoken Word.

*"Then God said,*
*'Let the earth bring forth grass,*
*the herb that yields seed,*
*and the fruit tree that yields fruit*
*according to its kind…"*
(Genesis 1:11-12)

Verse 20 goes on to say,

> *"Then God said,*
> *'Let the waters abound with an*
> *abundance of living creatures, and let*
> *birds fly above the earth across the face*
> *of the firmament of the heavens'."*

That is the reason for such immense variety and beauty in creation. In the midst of Adam and Eve's sin, God's original intent for mankind was always to have love, peace, and joy.

He gives us beauty for ashes!

# <u>Prayer for Day 26</u>

*Dear God,*

*Creator of heaven and earth how blessed I am to be surrounded by the beauty you have wrought. I am grateful for the stars, the moon, the sun, the oceans, the deserts, the mountains, and everything that makes up this beautiful world! For all of these things, I praise you!*

*In Jesus' name,*

*Amen.*

# What beauty have I witnessed in creation?

_____

_____

_____

_____

_____

_____

_____

_____

_____

_____

# Day 27

## CHANGE
## I Don't Like It!

One of the only constants in life is change because nothing remains the same forever. We'd love for the warmth and fuzziness to remain throughout the ages, or at least until we exit the planet, but that is not a realistic expectation. As long as Earth keeps spinning on its axis, things will change.

This is why we have four seasons, nine months of pregnancy, and different ages and stages of life.

Children leave the house at eighteen. Those children grow old, and eventually they move into the convalescent home at eighty.

Change, change, change—sometimes a friend, most of the time an enemy.

How do we cope with it?

Accept that change has no intention of leaving us any time soon. It shows up every morning, reminding us of its presence in the little and big things that occur every day. We don't have to like it, but let's face it with a smile and welcome all the lessons change teaches us as we  enter each season in the school of life.

## <u>Prayer for Day 27</u>

*Lord Jesus,*

*Who offers unwavering love and a supportive presence, please help me to accept the changes that are occurring in my life. Give me the confidence in your presence to see my potential in these new relationships and opportunities. These changes have made me very uncomfortable, and I need your guidance to keep from making decisions without forethought. Hastily made decisions might make me leave the path you have created for me. Help me to trust in you at all times, and in all things.*

*In Jesus' name,*

*Amen.*

# Lessons change has taught me:

_____

_____

_____

_____

_____

_____

_____

_____

# Day 28

Did You Know…?

Spanish as a second language is beautiful!

There was a woman who learned it by watching Mexican soap operas every day from Monday through Friday. Since she was consistent, she was able to have many intelligent conversations with Spanish speakers. She was a member of a Spanish-speaking church; and one day, she summoned the courage to preach to the congregation in their language.

Did this happen overnight? No, but she did not quit.

She dared to be bold; she set a goal for herself to master the Spanish language, and she did!

Try it; you may like it.

*The next two pages are from
"Day 28, Did You Know…?"
in Spanish, so you can give it a try!*

# Día 28

## Sabías…?

Es hermoso el segundo lenguaje del español.

Mi madré que lo aprendió viendo telenovelas mexicanas todos los días de lunes a viernes. Gracias a su coherencia, pudo tener muchas conversaciones inteligentes con hispanohablantes. Ella era miembro de una iglesia de habla hispana; y un día reunió el coraje para predicar a la congregación en su idioma.

¿Esto sucedió de la noche a la mañana? No, pero ella no renunció.

Se atrevió a ser audaz; se propuso como objetivo dominar el idioma español, ¡y lo logró!

Intentalo; puede que te guste.

## <u>Prayer for Day 28</u>
*(English version)*

*Dear Lord,*

*Please help me in pursuing my goals. I pray for the focus and perseverance to stick with this/these goal(s), even when it gets difficult.*

*In Jesus' name I pray,*

*Amen.*

# <u>Oración Para El Día 28</u>
## *(Versión en español)*

*Querido Señor,*

*Por favor ayúdame a alcanzar mis metas. Rezo por la concentración y la perseverancia para cumplir con este/estos objetivos, incluso cuando se vuelve difícil.*

*En el nombre de Jesús oro,*

*Amén.*

# What languages would I like to learn? How can I learn them?

_____

_____

_____

_____

_____

_____

_____

_____

_____

_____

# Day 29

## Thanks!

To be grateful on a daily basis is an attitude that must be cultivated. While it comes naturally to constantly complain as a result of our negative nature, we must choose to focus on all of the good things that are happening in and around us.

If we took the time to investigate how others are simply trying to survive day in and day out, that what we consider to be trash is another person's treasure, that we have food while others starve, that we have drinking water at our fingertips while others have to walk miles to find a water source, then—and only then—will we truly appreciate every blessing and keep the words *thank you* always at the tip of our tongues.

When we diligently count our many blessings, we'll be astonished beyond our wildest imagination to see ALL that the Lord has done.

# Prayer for Day 29

*Dear Lord,*

*Thank you for all the blessings you have given me. It is more than I could have ever hoped for. You have given me people who love me and look out for me. The family and friends you have provided bless me every day and lift me up in ways that allow me to focus on you. Thank you for keeping me safe and helping me make good choices. Thank you for keeping my loved ones safe. Please give me the forethought to show them every day how important they are to me and remind me how blessed I am to have you in my life.*

*In Jesus' name I pray,*

*Amen.*

# Blessings throughout my life:

_____

_____

_____

_____

_____

_____

_____

_____

_____

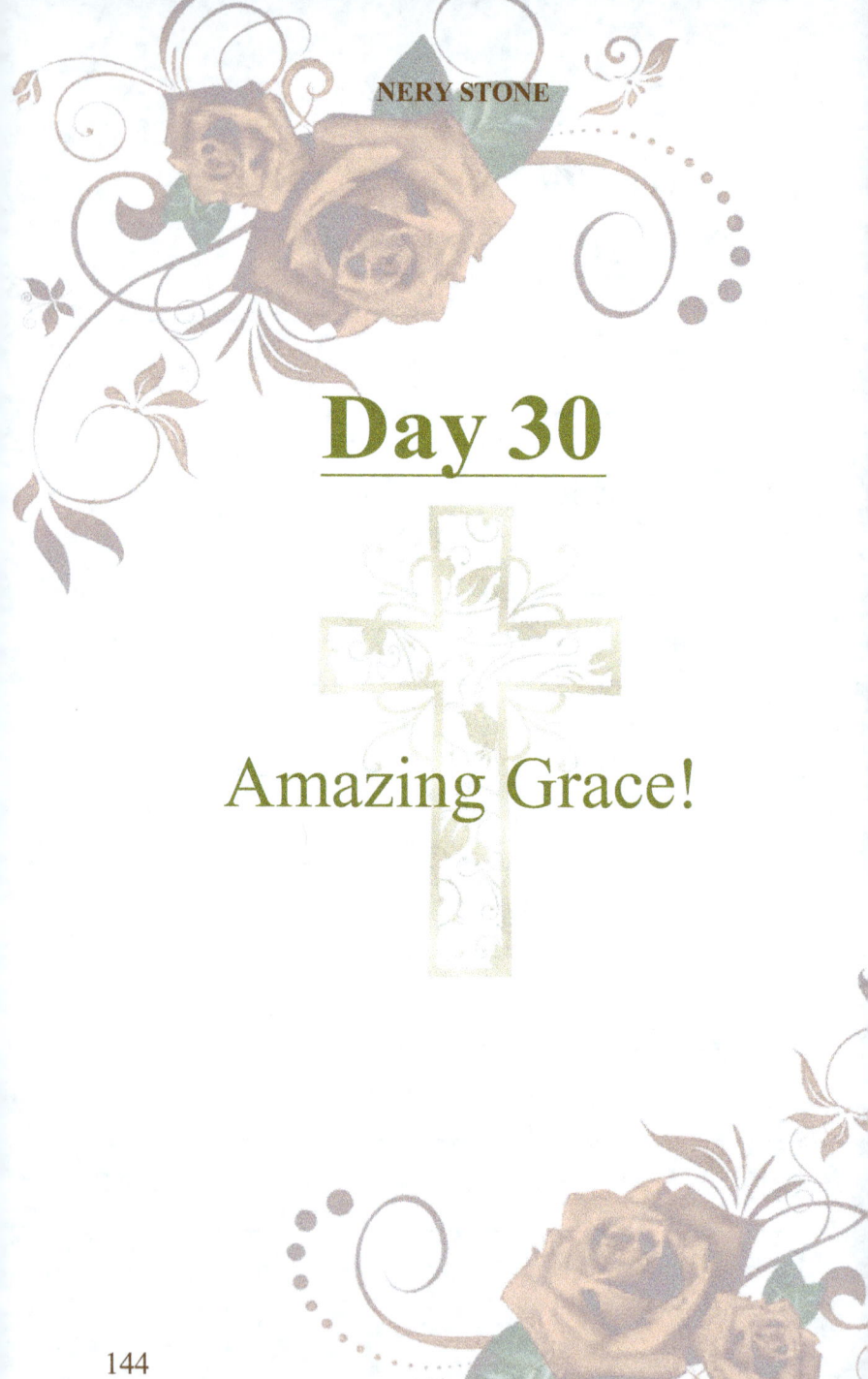

# Day 30

## Amazing Grace!

Unmerited favor, something bestowed upon us that we do not deserve and can never earn, flowing from God's heart just because He loves us…this is grace.

It cannot be described or explained; it is just there, fully accessible to those who love God and are called by His Name.

It keeps us humble, always seeking God's face before we seek His hand.

It keeps us looking up to where He is seated in the third heaven at the right hand of the Father, where He intercedes as our High Priest.

Grace - God's favor - is just one of the blessings we step into as children of the most high God!

Grace, we receive freely as a gift that also encourages us to extend it to others, especially when we have been offended by something they've said or done. Grace transforms us from the inside out; it helps us to walk the straight and narrow path. This blessing allows the words of our mouths and the thoughts that enter our minds to be pleasing to Him.

Let's show someone this same grace today.

## <u>Prayer for Day 30</u>

*Dear Lord,*

*I come before you with an open heart, asking for your grace to be a light in my life. I pray for the wisdom to understand the power of your grace, and to recognize it as the gift it is – not something to be earned. Please help me stay mindful of extending grace to others. Let me be forever grateful for your gift of grace.*

*In Jesus' name,*

*Amen.*

# How I can show grace to others today:

_____

_____

_____

_____

_____

_____

_____

_____

_____

_____

# Day 31

# Someone is Knocking at the Door

We are constantly busy: running here and there, talking on the phone, shopping at the grocery store, helping the family, being kind to our neighbors or anyone in need. Twenty-four hours in a day doesn't seem to be enough for all we have or want to get done (including the hours of rest our bodies need).

We get so stressed out in a frenzy, that we cannot hear the promptings of the Holy Spirit who longs to have fellowship with us, guide us, comfort us, and strengthen us.

The Word says in the Book of Revelation 3:20:

*"Here I am! I stand at the door and knock. If anyone hears my voice and opens the door, I will come in and eat with that person, and they with me."*

The Lord yearns for us to spend time with Him where He can speak to us through His Word. Here we can talk to him in prayer and worship.

Only what is done for Christ will last in this life because nothing else endures forever. Let's make time for what really counts—a relationship with God.

# <u>Prayer for Day 31</u>

*Dear Father God,*

*Please reveal any anxieties and concerns I have not given to you and lead me back to you. Through you, I know my mind and heart are clean. Please renew your spirit within me and bring me closer to you. Even when I am at my worst, and you feel so far away, in my heart I know your Spirit lives in me. Remind my soul of this truth.*

*In Jesus' name,*

*Amen.*

# Anxieties and concerns I carry around, and need to give to God:

_____

_____

_____

_____

_____

_____

_____

_____

_____

# About the Author

Nery Mariela Stone was born in the province of Colon, Republic of Panama. She is the youngest of three siblings. Her sister is Grace Beverly, and her brother was Rogelio Alberto. Due to a large age gap between Nery and her siblings, she often felt like an only child.

Nery attended St. Mary's Academy from primary to secondary school. Shortly after graduating from high school in the top of her class, Nery met her first husband. Given that he was in the Honduran military, she ended up moving to Honduras along with her parents Beresford Lloyd Stone and Ruth Elizabeth Skeete.

While in Honduras, Nery's first two children, Antonio and Ruth, were born. That marriage ended when her children were still very young, which led Nery to the United States with her parents and children. During that time, Nery rededicated her life to Christ

She retired in 2021 from one of the big four accounting firms located in Los Angeles, California. During retirement, Nery found passion in writing out the story of her life and several lessons learned along the way.

She hopes to continue impacting lives through this devotional long after she is gone…

# NERY STONE

# Acknowledgments

It is incredible that after a few years, I would meet Leanne Staback and come to find out her outstanding creative skills and passion. She took the initiative that most people never do and believed in this idea enough to help me bring this devotional to life.

When I think of wisdom, patience and divine miracles, my grandson, Gregory Jermaine is the man who comes to mind. For his young age, he carries such a testimony that most people would find unbelievable when I like to think of it as commendable.

Lastly, to my partner Tom Orsi, you were wonderful. Thank you for taking the time to teach me the ropes and have a successful career at the firm.

# NERY STONE